Sobriety Journal

THIS 90-DAY JOURNAL
BELONGS TO:

_____

_____

I am sober.

I am strong.

I am capable.

AND ABOVE ALL ELSE…

I am worth it!

I am worth it.

ONE DAY AT A TIME

My Story...

DESCRIBE MY JOURNEY SO FAR.

_____
_____
_____
_____
_____
_____
_____
_____
_____
_____
_____
_____
_____
_____
_____
_____
_____
_____
_____
_____
_____
_____
_____
_____
_____
_____
_____

DID I STAY SOBER TODAY?

I am worth it.

ONE DAY AT A TIME

My Rock Bottom...

DESCRIBE THE CATALYST FOR CHANGE.

_____
_____
_____
_____
_____
_____
_____
_____
_____
_____
_____
_____
_____
_____
_____
_____
_____
_____
_____
_____
_____
_____
_____
_____
_____

DID I STAY SOBER TODAY?

I am worth it.

My Hope & Dreams...

EXPLAIN WHY STAYING SOBER MEANS SO MUCH TO ME.

_____
_____
_____
_____
_____
_____
_____
_____
_____
_____
_____
_____
_____
_____
_____
_____
_____
_____
_____
_____
_____
_____
_____
_____
_____
_____

DID I STAY SOBER TODAY?

I am worth it.

The People That Matter...

DESCRIBE THE PEOPLE ROOTING FOR ME.

DID I STAY SOBER TODAY?

I am worth it.

Talk to my younger self

IF I KNEW THEN WHAT I KNOW NOW…

_____
_____
_____
_____
_____
_____
_____
_____
_____
_____
_____
_____
_____
_____
_____
_____
_____
_____
_____
_____
_____
_____
_____
_____
_____
_____

DID I STAY SOBER TODAY?

I am worth it.

What Inspires Me

WHAT KEEPS ME GOING…

DID I STAY SOBER TODAY?

I am worth it.

Being My True Self

DESCRIBE HOW I CAN BE MORE AUTHENTIC.

_____
_____
_____
_____
_____
_____
_____
_____
_____
_____
_____
_____
_____
_____
_____
_____
_____
_____
_____
_____
_____
_____
_____
_____

DID I STAY SOBER TODAY?

I am worth it.

Why I Matter

EXPLAIN WHY I BELIEVE IN MYSELF

_____
_____
_____
_____
_____
_____
_____
_____
_____
_____
_____
_____
_____
_____
_____
_____
_____
_____
_____
_____
_____
_____
_____

DID I STAY SOBER TODAY?

☐   ☐

I am worth it.

Critical Thoughts

WRITE MY CRITICAL THOUGHTS AND
RELEASE THEM FROM MY MIND & SPIRIT

_____
_____
_____
_____
_____
_____
_____
_____
_____
_____
_____
_____
_____
_____
_____
_____
_____
_____
_____
_____
_____
_____
_____
_____
_____

DID I STAY SOBER TODAY?

I am worth it.

ONE DAY AT A TIME

Recovery Plan

EXPLAIN HOW I PLAN TO BE SUCCESSFUL.

DID I STAY SOBER TODAY?

I am worth it.

ONE DAY AT A TIME

My Triggers

DESCRIBE MY TRIGGERS AND HOW I PLAN
TO AVOID THEM DURING RECOVERY

DID I STAY SOBER TODAY?

I am worth it.

My Addiction Shadow

DESCRIBE MY ADDICTION PERSONALITY.

DID I STAY SOBER TODAY?

I am worth it.

Lessons From Yesterday

DESCRIBE 3 THINGS I'VE LEARNED.

DID I STAY SOBER TODAY?

I am worth it.

Today's Affirmation

WRITE DOWN AN AFFIRMATION FOR THE DAY.

_____

_____

_____

_____

_____

_____

_____

_____

_____

_____

_____

_____

_____

_____

_____

_____

_____

_____

_____

_____

_____

_____

DID I STAY SOBER TODAY?

I am worth it.

ONE DAY AT A TIME

My Greatest Regrets

DESCRIBE MY GREATEST REGRETS FROM
PAST ACTIONS TAKEN WHEN NOT SOBER

DID I STAY SOBER TODAY?

I am worth it.

My Weaknesses

DESCRIBE WEAKNESSES OUTSIDE OF
GENERAL TRIGGERS THAT I MUST AVOID.

DID I STAY SOBER TODAY?

I am worth it.

ONE DAY AT A TIME

Positive Habit

DESCRIBE ONE POSITIVE HABIT I WOULD
LIKE TO BEGIN AS PART OF MY JOURNEY.

DID I STAY SOBER TODAY?

I am worth it.

My Best Traits

DESCRIBE 3 OF MY STRONGEST TRAITS

DID I STAY SOBER TODAY?

I am worth it.

Moment of Gratitude

DESCRIBE 2 THINGS I AM GRATEFUL FOR.

DID I STAY SOBER TODAY?

I am worth it.

No Time Like Today

DESCRIBE SOMETHING I WANT TO SAY TO SOMEONE THAT SHOULDN'T WAIT.

_____
_____
_____
_____
_____
_____
_____
_____
_____
_____
_____
_____
_____
_____
_____
_____
_____
_____
_____
_____
_____
_____
_____

DID I STAY SOBER TODAY?

I am worth it.

Give Myself a Break

DESCRIBE 2 WAYS I AM TOO HARD ON
MYSELF AND WHY I FEEL THAT WAY.

DID I STAY SOBER TODAY?

I am worth it.

A Day of Sobriety

DESCRIBE A TYPICAL DAY WHEN SOBER.

_____
_____
_____
_____
_____
_____
_____
_____
_____
_____
_____
_____
_____
_____
_____
_____
_____
_____
_____
_____
_____
_____
_____
_____

DID I STAY SOBER TODAY?

I am worth it.

ONE DAY AT A TIME

A Commitment To Myself

DESCRIBE HOW I WILL BE A BETTER
VERSION OF MYSELF TOMORROW.

DID I STAY SOBER TODAY?

I am worth it.

My Recovery Timeline

EXPLAIN MY RECOVERY TIMELINE,
INCLUDING WITH MY BEST MOMENTS.

DID I STAY SOBER TODAY?

I am worth it.

I will never surrender

DESCRIBE A RECENT MOMENT OF WEAKNESS
AND WHAT I DID TO OVERCOME IT.

_____
_____
_____
_____
_____
_____
_____
_____
_____
_____
_____
_____
_____
_____
_____
_____
_____
_____
_____
_____
_____
_____
_____

DID I STAY SOBER TODAY?

I am worth it.

My addiction in 10 words

DESCRIBE MY ADDICTION IN 10 WORDS.

DID I STAY SOBER TODAY?

I am worth it.

ONE DAY AT A TIME

A Distant Memory

DESCRIBE THE KEY AREAS OF MY LIFE
THAT ADDICTION HAS IMPACTED.

DID I STAY SOBER TODAY?

I am worth it.

ONE DAY AT A TIME

A brighter tomorrow

DESCRIBE HOW STAYING SOBER IS
IMPROVING MY LIFE.

_____
_____
_____
_____
_____
_____
_____
_____
_____
_____
_____
_____
_____
_____
_____
_____
_____
_____
_____
_____
_____
_____
_____
_____
_____

DID I STAY SOBER TODAY?

I am worth it.

Stronger than yesterday

EXPLAIN THE PLACES THAT I DRAW
STRENGTH FROM TO KEEP ON FIGHTING.

_____
_____
_____
_____
_____
_____
_____
_____
_____
_____
_____
_____
_____
_____
_____
_____
_____
_____
_____
_____
_____
_____
_____
_____

DID I STAY SOBER TODAY?

I am worth it.

ONE DAY AT A TIME

My own hero

DESCRIBE THE POSITIVE THINGS I FEEL
ABOUT MYSELF DURING THIS JOURNEY.

DID I STAY SOBER TODAY?

I am worth it.

ONE DAY AT A TIME

My Self Fulfillment

EXPLAIN HOW STAYING SOBER WILL
IMPROVE YOUR MENTAL HEALTH.

DID I STAY SOBER TODAY?

I am worth it.

ONE DAY AT A TIME

My Greatest Influence

DESCRIBE THE ONE PERSON WHO HAS THE
MOST INFLUENCE OVER ME.

DID I STAY SOBER TODAY?

I am worth it.

ONE DAY AT A TIME

The Missing Piece

DESCRIBE ONE THING I FEEL IS MISSING FROM MY LIFE.

DID I STAY SOBER TODAY?

I am worth it.

ONE DAY AT A TIME

My Ideal Day

DESCRIBE AN IDEAL DAY STAYING SOBER.

_____
_____
_____
_____
_____
_____
_____
_____
_____
_____
_____
_____
_____
_____
_____
_____
_____
_____
_____
_____
_____
_____
_____
_____
_____
_____

DID I STAY SOBER TODAY?

☐   ☐

I am worth it.

ONE DAY AT A TIME

My Daily Ritual

DESCRIBE MY MORNING, AFTERNOON AND
EVENING RITUAL THAT HELPS ME FOCUS.

DID I STAY SOBER TODAY?

I am worth it.

ONE DAY AT A TIME

My Daily Progress

CELEBRATE MY DAILY PROGRESS.

DID I STAY SOBER TODAY?

I am worth it.

ONE DAY AT A TIME

Dear Past Me...

WRITE A LETTER TO MY PAST SELF.

_____
_____
_____
_____
_____
_____
_____
_____
_____
_____
_____
_____
_____
_____
_____
_____
_____
_____
_____
_____
_____
_____
_____
_____
_____
_____

DID I STAY SOBER TODAY?

I am worth it.

ONE DAY AT A TIME

Dear Present Me...

WRITE A LETTER TO MY PRESENT SELF.

DID I STAY SOBER TODAY?

I am worth it.

ONE DAY AT A TIME

Dear Future Me...

WRITE A LETTER TO MY FUTURE SELF.

_____
_____
_____
_____
_____
_____
_____
_____
_____
_____
_____
_____
_____
_____
_____
_____
_____
_____
_____
_____
_____
_____
_____
_____

DID I STAY SOBER TODAY?

☐   ☐

I am worth it.

ONE DAY AT A TIME

To Those I Love The Most

WRITE A LETTER TO SOMEONE I LOVE.

DID I STAY SOBER TODAY?

I am worth it.

ONE DAY AT A TIME

A Learning Process

DESCRIBE WHAT I'VE LEARNED ABOUT
MYSELF DURING THIS JOURNEY.

DID I STAY SOBER TODAY?

I am worth it.

ONE DAY AT A TIME

Goodbye Letter

WRITE A GOODBYE LETTER TO SOMEONE I
HAVE TO LET GO OF TO STAY SOBER.

DID I STAY SOBER TODAY?

I am worth it.

ONE DAY AT A TIME

What Makes Me Smile ☺

WRITE DOWN THE THING THAT MAKE ME
SMILE AND AID IN MY RECOVERY.

DID I STAY SOBER TODAY?

I am worth it.

My Autobiography

WRITE DOWN A FEW THINGS I WOULD LOVE
TO READ IN MY AUTOBIOGRAPHY.

_____

_____

_____

_____

_____

_____

_____

_____

_____

_____

_____

_____

_____

_____

_____

_____

_____

_____

_____

_____

DID I STAY SOBER TODAY?

I am worth it.

ONE DAY AT A TIME

Confident Thoughts

WRITE ABOUT ONE MOMENT WHERE I FELT
THE MOST CONFIDENT DURING MY JOURNEY.

_____
_____
_____
_____
_____
_____
_____
_____
_____
_____
_____
_____
_____
_____
_____
_____
_____
_____
_____
_____
_____
_____
_____
_____

DID I STAY SOBER TODAY?

I am worth it.

My Fondest Memories

DESCRIBE 2 OF MY FONDEST MEMORIES.

_____
_____
_____
_____
_____
_____
_____
_____
_____
_____
_____
_____
_____
_____
_____
_____
_____
_____
_____
_____
_____
_____
_____
_____

DID I STAY SOBER TODAY?

☐   ☐

I am worth it.

Freedom Means...

WRITE DOWN WHAT THE WORD "FREEDOM" MEANS TO ME.

_____
_____
_____
_____
_____
_____
_____
_____
_____
_____
_____
_____
_____
_____
_____
_____
_____
_____
_____
_____
_____
_____
_____
_____

DID I STAY SOBER TODAY?

I am worth it.

ONE DAY AT A TIME

Last Mistake

DESCRIBE MY LAST MISTAKE AND WHAT I
LEARNED FROM IT.

DID I STAY SOBER TODAY?

I am worth it.

ONE DAY AT A TIME

Tomorrow's Goal

WRITE DOWN A GOAL FOR TOMORROW AND
HOW I PLAN TO ACCOMPLISH IT.

_____

_____

_____

_____

_____

_____

_____

_____

_____

_____

_____

_____

_____

_____

_____

_____

_____

_____

_____

_____

_____

_____

DID I STAY SOBER TODAY?

I am worth it.

When No One's Watching

DESCRIBE HOW I PLAN TO LIVE MY BEST
LIFE LIKE NO ONE IS WATCHING.

DID I STAY SOBER TODAY?

I am worth it.

ONE DAY AT A TIME

My Greatest Fears

DESCRIBE MY GREATEST FEARS.

_____
_____
_____
_____
_____
_____
_____
_____
_____
_____
_____
_____
_____
_____
_____
_____
_____
_____
_____
_____
_____
_____
_____
_____
_____

DID I STAY SOBER TODAY?

I am worth it.

My One True Wish

DESCRIBE MY ONE TRUE WISH FOR MYSELF.

DID I STAY SOBER TODAY?

I am worth it.

What Recovery Means

DESCRIBE WHAT RECOVERY MEANS TO ME.

DID I STAY SOBER TODAY?

I am worth it.

I Couldn't Live Without

DESCRIBE ONE THING I COULDN'T LIVE
WITHOUT AND WHY IT MEANS SO MUCH.

DID I STAY SOBER TODAY?

I am worth it.

ONE DAY AT A TIME

If My Body Could Talk

DESCRIBE WHAT MY BODY WOULD SAY IF IT
COULD TALK.

DID I STAY SOBER TODAY?

I am worth it.

ONE DAY AT A TIME

To My Addiction...

WRITE A LETTER TO MY ADDICTION.

_____

_____

_____

_____

_____

_____

_____

_____

_____

_____

_____

_____

_____

_____

_____

_____

_____

_____

_____

_____

_____

_____

_____

_____

_____

DID I STAY SOBER TODAY?

[ ]   [ ]

I am worth it.

ONE DAY AT A TIME

If I wasn't in recovery

DESCRIBE WHERE I'D BE IN MY LIFE IF I
WASN'T IN RECOVERY.

_____
_____
_____
_____
_____
_____
_____
_____
_____
_____
_____
_____
_____
_____
_____
_____
_____
_____
_____
_____
_____
_____
_____
_____
_____

DID I STAY SOBER TODAY?

I am worth it.

ONE DAY AT A TIME

What I want them to know

DESCRIBE WHAT I WANT OTHERS TO KNOW
ABOUT ME WHEN MEETING NEW FRIENDS.

DID I STAY SOBER TODAY?

I am worth it.

My Happiest Moment

DESCRIBE ONE OF MY HAPPIEST MOMENTS
FROM THE PAST YEAR.

DID I STAY SOBER TODAY?

I am worth it.

Why I'm An Addict

DESCRIBE WHAT I FEEL LED ME TO ADDICTION.

DID I STAY SOBER TODAY?

I am worth it.

Short-Term Goals

WRITE DOWN MY SHORT-TERM GOALS.

DID I STAY SOBER TODAY?

I am worth it.

Long-Term Goals

WRITE DOWN MY LONG-TERM GOALS.

DID I STAY SOBER TODAY?

I am worth it.

ONE DAY AT A TIME

Proud of Myself

DESCRIBE ONE THING I AM MOST PROUD OF.

_____
_____
_____
_____
_____
_____
_____
_____
_____
_____
_____
_____
_____
_____
_____
_____
_____
_____
_____
_____
_____
_____
_____
_____
_____
_____

DID I STAY SOBER TODAY?

I am worth it.

Through Dark Times

DESCRIBE ONE THING I WILL HOLD ONTO
DURING THE DARKEST TIMES.

DID I STAY SOBER TODAY?

I am worth it.

ONE DAY AT A TIME

My Personal Worries

EXPLAIN ONE THING THAT WORRIES ME AND
CAUSES ME STRESS.

_____
_____
_____
_____
_____
_____
_____
_____
_____
_____
_____
_____
_____
_____
_____
_____
_____
_____
_____
_____
_____
_____
_____
_____
_____

DID I STAY SOBER TODAY?

I am worth it.

Unpacking The Past

WRITE ABOUT THE HIGHLIGHTS OF MY PAST
AS WELL AS THE DARKEST DAYS.

_____

_____

_____

_____

_____

_____

_____

_____

_____

_____

_____

_____

_____

_____

_____

_____

_____

_____

_____

_____

_____

_____

_____

_____

DID I STAY SOBER TODAY?

☐   ☐

I am worth it.

ONE DAY AT A TIME

Wish upon a star

IF I COULD WISH FOR ANYTHING, WHAT
WOULD IT BE?

_____

_____

_____

_____

_____

_____

_____

_____

_____

_____

_____

_____

_____

_____

_____

_____

_____

_____

_____

_____

_____

_____

_____

_____

DID I STAY SOBER TODAY?

I am worth it.

10 Ways My Life is Better

WRITE DOWN 10 WAYS STAYING SOBER HAS
IMPROVED MY LIFE.

DID I STAY SOBER TODAY?

I am worth it.

Progress, Not Perfection

DESCRIBE WHY PROGRESS IS MOST
IMPORTANT, NOT PERFECTION.

DID I STAY SOBER TODAY?

I am worth it.

Tired, So Tired

WRITE ABOUT ONE THING I'M TIRED OF.

_____

_____

_____

_____

_____

_____

_____

_____

_____

_____

_____

_____

_____

_____

_____

_____

_____

_____

_____

_____

_____

_____

_____

_____

DID I STAY SOBER TODAY?

☐　　　☐

I am worth it.

ONE DAY AT A TIME

5 Years From Now

DESCRIBE WHERE I SEE MYSELF IN FIVE
YEARS FROM NOW.

_____
_____
_____
_____
_____
_____
_____
_____
_____
_____
_____
_____
_____
_____
_____
_____
_____
_____
_____
_____
_____
_____
_____
_____
_____

DID I STAY SOBER TODAY?

I am worth it.

Who I Admire Most

DESCRIBE THE PERSON I ADMIRE MOST AND
WHY I LOOK UP TO THEM.

_____
_____
_____
_____
_____
_____
_____
_____
_____
_____
_____
_____
_____
_____
_____
_____
_____
_____
_____
_____
_____
_____
_____
_____

DID I STAY SOBER TODAY?

☐   ☐

I am worth it.

ONE DAY AT A TIME

My Current Outlook

DESCRIBE MY CURRENT OUTLOOK ON LIFE.

DID I STAY SOBER TODAY?

I am worth it.

Unconditional Love

DESCRIBE WHAT THE WORDS
"UNCONDITIONAL LOVE" MEANS TO ME.

DID I STAY SOBER TODAY?

I am worth it.

Questions I ask myself

WRITE DOWN 3 QUESTIONS I OFTEN FIND
MYSELF ASKING MYSELF.

_____
_____
_____
_____
_____
_____
_____
_____
_____
_____
_____
_____
_____
_____
_____
_____
_____
_____
_____
_____
_____
_____
_____
_____
_____
_____

DID I STAY SOBER TODAY?

I am worth it.

Answers I need

ANSWER THE 3 QUESTIONS FROM
YESTERDAY.

_____
_____
_____
_____
_____
_____
_____
_____
_____
_____
_____
_____
_____
_____
_____
_____
_____
_____
_____
_____
_____
_____
_____
_____
_____
_____
_____

DID I STAY SOBER TODAY?

I am worth it.

What Paradise Looks Like

DESCRIBE THE PERFECT LIFE.

_____
_____
_____
_____
_____
_____
_____
_____
_____
_____
_____
_____
_____
_____
_____
_____
_____
_____
_____
_____
_____
_____
_____
_____
_____

DID I STAY SOBER TODAY?

I am worth it.

Self-Love Today & Always

LEARNING TO TAKE CARE OF MYSELF IS A
PRIORITY. DESCRIBE HOW I CAN DO THAT.

DID I STAY SOBER TODAY?

I am worth it.

ONE DAY AT A TIME

Letting Go

DESCRIBE AN EXPERIENCE I AM HAVING
TROUBLE LETTING GO OF.

DID I STAY SOBER TODAY?

I am worth it.

ONE DAY AT A TIME

The Lies I've Told

WRITE DOWN SOME OF THE LIES MY
ADDICTION HAS TOLD.

DID I STAY SOBER TODAY?

I am worth it.

ONE DAY AT A TIME

The Sober Version of Me

DESCRIBE THE SOBER VERSION OF MYSELF.

_____
_____
_____
_____
_____
_____
_____
_____
_____
_____
_____
_____
_____
_____
_____
_____
_____
_____
_____
_____
_____
_____
_____
_____

DID I STAY SOBER TODAY?

I am worth it.

Overcoming Insecurities

DESCRIBE MY GREATEST INSECURITY AND
HOW I CAN OVERCOME IT

DID I STAY SOBER TODAY?

I am worth it.

ONE DAY AT A TIME

My Growth

DESCRIBE HOW I FEEL I'VE GROWN OVER
THE LAST 85 DAYS

DID I STAY SOBER TODAY?

I am worth it.

True Acceptance

DESCRIBE WHAT ACCEPTANCE MEANS TO ME.

DID I STAY SOBER TODAY?

I am worth it.

ONE DAY AT A TIME

What I Need Help With

DESCRIBE WHAT I NEED THE MOST HELP
WITH AND HOW I CAN GET IT.

DID I STAY SOBER TODAY?

I am worth it.

ONE DAY AT A TIME

Coping Mechanisms

DESCRIBE SOME OF MY COPING
MECHANISMS.

DID I STAY SOBER TODAY?

I am worth it.

Saying Yes More Often

WRITE DOWN A LIST OF EVERYTHING IN MY
LIFE I WANT TO SAY YES TO.

DID I STAY SOBER TODAY?

I am worth it.

Putting Myself First

WRITE DOWN A LIST OF ALL THE THINGS I
WANT TO LEARN TO SAY NO TO.

DID I STAY SOBER TODAY?

I am worth it.

ONE DAY AT A TIME

Notes

I am worth it.

ONE DAY AT A TIME

Notes

I am worth it.

ONE DAY AT A TIME

Notes

I am worth it.

ONE DAY AT A TIME

Notes

I am worth it.

ONE DAY AT A TIME

Notes

I am worth it.

ONE DAY AT A TIME

Notes

I am worth it.

ONE DAY AT A TIME

Notes

I am worth it.

ONE DAY AT A TIME

Notes

I am worth it.

ONE DAY AT A TIME

Notes

I am sober.

I am strong.

I am capable.

AND ABOVE ALL ELSE…

I am worth it!

Made in United States
Troutdale, OR
12/29/2024

27413585R00056